The Wood That Will Be Used

Also by Mary Leader

Red Signature
The Penultimate Suitor
Beyond the Fire
She Lives There Still
The Distaff Side

The
Wood
That
Will Be
Used

Mary
LEADER

SHEARSMAN BOOKS

First published in the United Kingdom in 2024 by
Shearsman Books
PO Box 4239
SWINDON
SN3 9FN

Shearsman Books Ltd Registered Office
30-31 St. James Place, Mangotsfield, Bristol BS16 9JB
(this address not for correspondence)

www.shearsman.com

ISBN 978-184861-925-8

ACKNOWLEDGMENTS

Cimarron Review: 'Circles'; 'Help-Stone';
'The Methodist Ministry of Samuel Walsh Franklin';
Grasslands Review: 'Us Girls';
Image: 'Double Visitation';
Shearsman: 'Alternative Canticle of Mary';
'Spire and Dove'; 'The Sun'; 'Yankee Doodle Dandy';
Tears in the Fence: 'Earthshine's Lament'

Help-meets of my late poems:
Donald Platt & Margaret Ann Wadleigh:
champions both.
Two more: *Tony Frazer & Tony Roberts*: each
willing to exercise his genius on my behalf.
My faith-carriers: *Rosemary Ford, Amy Gardner,
Wallis Ohl, Pamela Wallace, and Charles Woltz.*
And readers heart-closest always:
Neal Leader, Sara Leader, Edward Leader.

CONTENTS

Prologue

Although he lost his religious faith towards the end of his five-year residence in London in the 1860s, Thomas Hardy remained 'churchy' to use his own term, until the end of his life. He was particularly drawn to churchyards, and to the rituals and physical processes involved in church burial. In a late poem, 'The Six Boards', he even broods on the current state of the wood that will be used to make the coffin in which he will himself soon be interred.

— Mark Ford
Thomas Hardy: Half a Londoner
Cambridge, Mass. & London, Eng.
Belknap Press of Harvard U P, 2016.

Note: Thomas Hardy's poem titled 'The Six Boards' governs the structure of this book. The book is organized into six sections, called "boards." Beginning with the second one, each board is introduced by a stanza of the Hardy poem, which is further set out in its entirety in the appendix to this book for the reader's reference.

First Board

By way of orientation, I have written:
When the moon reaches crescent phase,
which is to say, when the sun sets
on the moon's earth-facing side,
then that dark side may be visible
to us, illumined by sunlight reflected
          from our own planet.

Astronomers call the phenomenon
"earthshine." Leonardo da Vinci
labeled it the moon's "ashen glow."
Folklore has depicted it as "the old moon
in the new moon's arms," or in another
variant, "the new moon with the old
          moon in her arm."

That figure of speech appears within
the traditional ballad of Sir Patrick Spens,
skipper *par excellence* of a sea-worthy boat.*
But before Spens sets sail, one of his crew
reports observing a dread sign, known since
before any of them were born, as portending
          a deadly storm at sea.

"For late yestreen," says he (which in Scots
dialect means yesterday evening), "I saw
the new muin wi' the auld muin in hir arme."
Not that the warning stopped Sir Patrick
from attempting the crossing (as ordered
by his King) — over the chill North Sea,
          for Norway bound.

The English and Scottish Popular Ballads, compiled by Francis James Child; "Sir
Patrick Spens" is Child Ballad No. 58.

Earthshine's Lament

Thus I arrive — where turf gives way to thicket —

Graveyard's edge. Who causes movement — wind merely?

Does twilight, alone, enliven these shadows? —

Crook'd, or straight — fox's legs, or scrawny saplings.

Overhead — between pale coasts of two dark clouds

Drifts *the new muin wi' the auld muin in hir arme.*

For you, Patrick Spens — catastrophic omen.

For you, Lyrical Mother — grand idiom.

Sly moon, you scoff, embezzle gleams from polished

Granite. Rain, you send down leaves, dead and dying,

Umber and wet, to weight the ground like lead-lined

Aprons for x-rays, and when rain morphs into

Percussive sleet, the leaf-mats act as detached

Drumheads that timpani players have soaked for

Flexibility, to be tuned by torquing

Gauges, bouncing strikes of felt-headed mallets.

Stalwart Mother, insects navigate your hair.

You envy them. And snakes. And bats in true flight.

Voles. No matter how deep, or how late into,

The winter, voles couch in their holes, in contact

With each other. Muscles surrounding their eyes

Gradually release their guard, but snap wide

At approach, stealthy predator's sound or smell.

As intaglio involves scratching metal

To raise burrs to grip ink, so rot claws at snarled

Amaranth tubes of digestion, of heart-valves.

Next comes mold's palette — green and black and cyan —

To reduce to powder your shroud, pock your face,

Smear your every careful comma. Where once you

Suffered your empty gut, star-finned minerals

Nick your ribs. All manner of molecule grows —

Granular, unstalled — all displacing. Your hands,

The digits first, are by decay — decay! — are

By Decay's snuffling lowered mouth fondled — then —

Devoured. Palms. Oh, twin wrists like weathered turnips.

There — you go. When I — take my place in the new

Row of plots here, I think I will hear, right through

Occupied soil, your fierce subliminal roar.

Shape-Shift

Figurine of a Man
Undergoing Transformation
reads the museum
exhibit placard.
The man, who has
achondroplasia,
looks to be putting on
a fur coat,
turning, I surmise,
into, well?
a bear? until
I undergo reading
the rest of the placard.
Transformation into
Some Small Rodent.
Mayan. Yucatán
Peninsula. Yellow
Clay. All right, then,
into some
small yellow
rodent, formerly
quick to scurry
in dust, to shelter
in scrub.
The artifact also
functioned as *A*
Ceremonial Whistle.
Instrument capable
of swirling breath
into sheer
ecstasy. Now
it abides, soundless,

immobile, remaindered,
mounted upon
a Lucite cube.
But this mammal
could just as well be
taking off
the fur coat,
am I wrong?
Figurine of
a Rodent Undergoing
Transformation into
Some Small Man.
In either direction,
I observe the eyes,
ovalled and bulged
in pain, one being
not yet released
to another.

Alternative Canticle of Mary

And Marie said, My soule doth magnifie the Lord.
— Luke 1:46 [King James Version, 1611]

Et ait Maria: Magnificat anima mea Dominum
— Luke 1:46 [The Vulgate, trans. Jerome of Stridon, 405]

~~Magnificat~~ Diminuit
anima mea Dominum. *My soule*
doth diminish the Lord.

Too late
ever again
to turn my forehead to the sky

with my eyes
closed to receive
what?

÷

My purview, downcast,
consists wholly of wheel-gouged
roads, whether

these ruts stream
sick with flood,
or, like eye-slits in merciless

sun, bake,
bandageless
and blind.

÷

I did ask
God for it, for the
        termination. Asked by rescinding

my availability
as vessel.
        What could God even say?

Not much,
considering that God's
        own spokesman, Gabriel,

while explaining
how I was to fall pregnant,
        made it quite clear

that my heartfelt
consent
        was of the essence.

÷

Stupid girl.
Blithe, stupid girl.
        I spared

a human-to-be
the crux of
        a death-to-be.

I spared myself
what I believed
        at the time

was the very worst
pain possible
                on this earth.

                        ÷

        Childbirth? Hardly.
Much worse.
                To stand powerless

        by
as the flesh of my flesh
                grows up to encounter

        evil,
incarnate
                and equipped.

                        ÷

        To stand there
without adequate language, without
                any language, as their screams rend

        all the air.
Fingers, ears, lips, easily removed.
                Tenderness,

        flayed.
Raped, castrated,
                laughed at.

                        ÷

Or buried standing within
the ground, up to the neck,
                as rocks

        hurled overhand
in increasing frenzy
                strike

        the face
the scalp
                the scalp again

        again the face
again again
                the cranium.

                        ÷

        Avoided, personally.
Even so,
                stupid decision.

        Stupid
but blithe,
                I tell you

        I did not feel
momentous.
                My history shall not survive me,

        my mark an M carved
in an utterly inaccessible cave:
                my mind.

                        ÷

In my dotage, by touch,
by compulsion,
            I collect

        meaningless
linen, meaningless
            parchment,

        bread, wax, meaningless all,
oil, dew,
            clay.

        I forbid
myself
            to pray.

                    ÷

        Having foreclosed
miracle,
            having precluded resurrection,

        I proceed
to the true
            worst pain possible:

        knowledge
that in the official chain,
            as proposed by God via Gabriel,

        had I stayed willing,
I would have outlived
            the child-birth pain,

the witness-to-torture pain,
even unto
death on the cross,

and on this earth
would have been able
triumphantly to say:

Now, I stand up and depart,
for the Word I conceived
is not in this grave.

÷

What now
would I give? *Would?* There is
no *would*, nothing I *could*

give in exchange
for five minutes, for twenty seconds, for one,
of being

that young mother-a-common,
walking the pathway
on her healthy feet,

smiling
at her secret
fecundity.

Second Board

Six boards belong to me:
I do not know where they may be;
If growing green, or lying dry
         In a cockloft nigh.

Help-Stone

Then Samuel took a single stone, and set it up between Mizpah and Shen, and he called its name Eben-Ezer and he said, "As far as here has the LORD helped us."*
— 1 Samuel 7:12 [The Hebrew Bible, trans. Robert Alter, 2018]

A. Observations of a Know-it-all

Where eulogists are guided principally
by anti-liturgical pro-congregational
feeling, in other words, in, let us say,
the Church-of-Christ tradition of speaking
off the cuff with a few customary tropes

thrown in, more as transition than content,
and where, in addition, the departed has not
yet managed to be buried or scattered, but,
has gotten so far as the coffin or the urn,
it may be in the nature of extemporaneous

mourning to shift around, quite a lot, as to
1. personal pronouns, e.g. I you he/she we
you they, 2. then, in the case of the second-
person singular you, as to the identity of
the addressee whether visible or invisible,

and, 3. in especial, as to the tenses of verbs,
a usage that makes perfect sense, because
at the locus for this category of speech-act,
during the minutes it lasts, the future is
acutely present and so, likewise, is the past.

*In Hebrew, "eben" means stone and "ezer" means helper

19

B. Example of a Eulogy

Good Morning!

My name is Ron Ellis and I am here representing the family of Lee Ellis, my father. We are here to celebrate his life. And it was a good life.

Praise God!

Our father was very organized. Loved organization. And he always had sage advice. Right, Tom? Sage advice and it is always right on point. And he is never shy about giving it to you! Lord, have mercy.

Dad, you were a hero in World War II in the Philippine Islands. You were awarded a Bronze Star for your bravery. You had scars on your body from knives and bayonet wounds from hand-to-hand combat with the enemy.

We are celebrating your life and your release to God. Praise God! Oh, Dad. We love you so, Dad. You are a man of immense character. And you are also a character. You appeal to a wide audience, Lee Ellis.

His full name is Norman Lee Ellis. He liked to go by Lee. But when we were kids, there was this song called Norman and it went Nor-man oo-wa oo-wa oo-waa Nor-man my luh-ove and we would would sing it to him and he would get all mad. But we had fun, we really did. Praise God. I truly love you, Dad.

Heavenly Father, as your dearly beloved Son taught us, to those whom much is given, much is expected. My father's intellect was great. His gift of intuition was immense.

Immense, Lord. And it was a gift he used wisely. Praise God His miracles to perform. This is the day that the Lord has made.

On this past Wednesday, Dad, Mother, and I had a prayer at noon. We had lunch and shortly thereafter Dad died in my arms. I held, Dad died . . .

in my arms, and . . . sorry.

And it was appropriate because he held his dad whenever his dad died. And Father . . .

Father, I just really and truly did love this man, Norman Lee Ellis. But Father, we know that he is with you now and with Bapo and Grandmother and Aunt Doris and all the others that have passed over and probably they're having a big fish-fry up there and I betcha ten dollars she brought her peach cobbler. Debby Sue, I hope you still have that recipe.

What?

Oh, okay.

Now let us open our hymnbook and sing Dad's favorite hymn. Please turn to page, what page is it on?

Oh, okay. It's hymn number two-twenty-six. 2-2-6. Wait, let me get my glasses on.

*C. Dad's Favorite Hymn**
(Selected Verses)

"Here I'll raise my ebenezer
Here by Thy great help I've come;
And I hope by Thy good pleasure
Safely to arrive at home."

"Come, my Lord, no longer tarry,
Take my ransomed soul away;
Send thine angels now to carry
Me to realms of endless day."

* "Come, Thou Fount of Ev'ry Blessing"
Written 1758
Text Robert Robinson
Meter 8:7:8:7
Melody Anonymous "Nettleton"; Wyeth's Repository of Sacred Music

The Senescence and Death of Hugh Galbraith, Late of Sir Albert Coyningham's Regiment of Dragoons ["Enniskilleners"]

|

It was resolved to attack the party
which Sutherland had left behind

|

in Béal Tairbirt. When within two
miles of the town, the dragoons

|

of both parties came in sight of
each other. After an exchange

|

|When does it happen,
|this further twisting

|

|of his spine? By day?
|since in dreams nightly,

|

|league upon league,
|he's still a fit rider.

|

of shots, the horse of the enemy
were driven back; the Enniskillen

|

horse, surrounding the church
and churchyard, kept them there till

|

the foot came forward and secured
the building. |

|

|
|Dawn, as it nears, reveals
|phantoms, flitting
|
|tree to tree to tree
|on his property.
|

Conditions of surrender |
were: That their lives should be

|

spared but the common soldiers
should be stripped of their coats.

|
|He much welcomes
|a fire,
|
|and to tend it,
|

The officers were not included

|

in this ignominious stipulation
and kept their money up to £10 each.

|
|Mari-Ailis.
|
|Window-frost,
|as if mending,
|
|melts in runnels,
|his eyesight too watery
|
|to perceive them.
|In his shaving basin
|

|

Almost three hundred prisoners were taken,
and in addition, seven hundred muskets, two

|

|he finds red
|residue, not iodine

|

barrels of powder, fifty-nine dragoon horses
and all accoutrements belonging to them,

|

|from the quack's bag,
|staining the porcelain,

|

as many red coats as served for two
companies, twenty horse-loads of biscuit,

|

fifty barrels of flour, a hundred of wheat
and some malt. This valuable plunder,

|

|but blood-tears from
|a fiend of some incarnadine

|

|ilk. His stallion canters;
|he'll not be reined in.

|

except the horses, was conveyed by
boat over Lough Erne to Enniskillen.

|

|Full-on gallop through arteries
|choked with woodbine.

|

Double Mirror

Some morning
in my trip midway in my life at a rest stop on Interstate-40,
      in the ladies' room,

there was this old woman, who could barely stand,
      who had to lean
on a toilet stall's none-too-steady door jamb, her hair cut

      short like that
of an old-time man of labor, smoking shakily, waiting for
      whomever

was inside the stall, whose name this elderly woman said,
      who answered
"Just a sec, Memaw" in an Okie accent a degree or two

      twangier than
my own. The cigarette between nicotine-stained fingers
      burned down;

it was worrisome; I wished the girl she was waiting for
      would hurry; good,
the cigarette dropped harmlessly to the concrete floor.

      My main
preoccupation, however, was not with them but with
      myself *qua*

poet. Facebook had yet to be launched but at that age
      I'd have been all
over it: "Fantastic news, ya'll!! *Snowy Egret* picked up

2 of my haiku!!!!"
That trip was, let me reflect, 1998. My front-of-mind
    "goal" in that restroom

was to "capture" in words the "essence" of my erstwhile
    haunt, Lake Thunderbird.
Truth be told, my poem was about nothing so much as

    trying to wow
whatever cute guy I'd filled in the blank with to be
    my muse that mid-

life year. Oh for God's sake; why be coy now? That was
    Rick Fogarty.
I was delighted in particular by my epiphanic closure:

    "The boats did
tame my eyes." Rick Fogarty was a bit of a — quite a bit
    of a — poseur.

Bostonian sporting Irish forebears by pronouncing "chune"
    for "tune" and
"tin" for "thin," which I aped. Entoirly. The 1900s saw,

    in fact, very few
sailboats in slow distant beauty on Lake Thunderbird.
    And it wasn't that

I disparaged the dominant fast and raucous motor boats —
    only that
it never occurred to me to write about them. Oklahoma

    has a red tinge
to its dirt due to ferrous oxide and therefore a faint
    rustiness to its lakes

but I wanted the lake in my poem to be gray, which I
        spelled, of course,
g-r-e-y. At the present juncture, using my imaginary

        memory, I decide
one sail was royal blue, or purple, one pink and yellow;
        classic white;

flame of sunset; black of myth, but so what? I'd have done
        far better to jot
down or even honestly remember (and for the life of me

        I cannot) the first
name (clearly I heard it) spoken by that bony old lady to
        her granddaughter,

who (listen) . . . finishes pissing, flushes the powerful
        public toilet
and emerges, startling me in her resemblance to my young

        self. Red hair,
round face, more smiles than frowns, such sweet freckles.
        Now, *instanter*,

the pair, again, departs my eyes forever. This poem closes:
        At a rest stop on
I-40, on such a day, in such an Autumn, a young woman

        of Irish descent
supports, gently, by the elbow, one senior American citizen
        in her withering.

Third Board

Some morning I shall claim them,
And who may then possess will aim them
To bring me those boards I need
*   With thoughtful speed.*

Us Girls

My Granny actually did get caught with nothing
in her refrigerator other than Sara Lee Cheesecake.
"Well no wonder she's sick," said every one of
her offspring. One time one of her daughters-in-law
berated her mercilessly, unceasingly, for an hour,
for a whole two days, off and on, because the yogurt
the daughter-in-law had taken from the fridge
(called icebox) — "I thought I'd have a nice yogurt
for dessert" (justified) — was green moldy!

Green Moldy! Green Moldy! Green Moldy!
You'd think she'd never have been so shocked.
Did I say "For Chrissakes, Ida, she's an old lady"?
No, this was Aunt Ida, one of the army of women
of an age to wear eyeglasses after the War, well,
a bit later, when they, the glasses, were cat-like.
No use crying over when rouge was rouge, not yet
"blusher" or "blush" let alone "bronzer." "I lack my
vanella ahs crame," in my native tongue, translates:

"I like to enjoy, habitually, an individual serving
of ice cream, preferably vanilla, not to be shared
with anybody." We say "daughter-in-laws," not
"daughters-in-law." But yes, I like vanilla ice cream,
yes-sir-ee-bob-cat-tail. Here's the thing, Granny.
If I abandoned my role — skinny, girdled, divorced,
and dolled up — I'd have dessert "ever damn day,"
not think of marrying — "no nay never / no more" —
my personal mother-in-law having "passed away."

Yankee Doodle Dandy*

Max Goldberg was born, family lore had it,
on the 4th of July. The year, by contrast,
was known for certain: 1905. Last I heard,
they threw him a big party in Miami Beach.
A hundred years and counting — counting,
it turned out, to 103. It's a piece of cake
from my comfy chair to google stats like that.
I grow old I grow gray. Very old and totally
gray, well, almost totally. Sorry. Already,
I've digressed. Not long after Rose Goldberg
died, I penned — I used to dig words like
"penned" — "So how is Max doing?"
in an email to a grandchild of his. "Pretty well,"
corresponded the grandchild, elaborating:
"I asked him if there were any activities
at the synagogue he might enjoy. He replied
that at his age, he has no desire or need for friends.
I understand. What's he going to do? Play cards
with other old men?" Beryl tried to coax him
into polo shirts in kindergarten colors. That
was never gonna fly. He liked oxford-cloth
shirts, button-down collars. He liked
the men around him to be wearing ties,
though seldomer and seldomer did they.

* * *

*Popular song by George M. Cohan in 1904. Lyrics include:
"I'm a Yankee doodle dandy / Yankee Doodle do or die
A real live nephew of my Uncle Sam / Born on the Fourth of July"
"Father's name was Hezikiah / Mother's name was Ann Maria
Yanks through and through / Red, white and blue"

When I was at Brandeis, I knew a Bulgarian
who pronounced "category" with the same rhythm
that my British Editor, or any Briton for that matter,
would, stressing not syllables 1 and 3 about equally
but syllable 2 — "contrÓversy" — "catÉgory" —
which I prefer. I thought about the catégory
of Found Poetry. I'd been visiting my own four
dead grandparents, researching games circa 1955 —
Mid-century Modern! Design Within Reach™ —
specifically a Parker-Brothers card-game called Rook.
I took notes. I did write about that game, inter alia.
You can find the piece, if you want to. Look
in my spare bedroom for a black spring-back
binder neatly labeled with white vinyl letters —
DISTAFF WORKSHEETS — except the letters
are in the font Helvetica, not my favorite Williams
Caslon. In the alternative, why not wend
your way to Shrivenham, in Oxfordshire?
Inquire therein for my editor, Tony Frazer.
Surely any villager will know which house.
If you're not going to be in the U. K. anytime soon,
you may find a portion of the work, originally
a triptych, by going online and ordering
Mr. Frazer's magazine, *Shearsman*, no. 123/124.

                              * * *

I pressed against T. F.'s window during one of
his Septembers my trio in a word docx. He took
Part I — 'How Methodists, Who Don't Believe
in it, Play Cards.' And he took Part II — 'How
Catholics, Who Do Believe in it, Play Cards.'
But he sheared off Part III — 'Permissible for All:
Old Maid, Go Fish, Authors.' To this day,
I go back and forth as to what I think about
Part III. It is a process poem, displaying a bunch

of material in the found-poetry catégory,
derived from an experimental form of Solitaire —
did you know that in England, Solitaire is called
Patience? — that I devised using an outdated deck
of the game "Authors." Its burden was to say
I wish my mother's poems lived in the world
instead of in a robin's-egg-blue checkered binder
in my spare bedroom. Now my own Part III
resides unpublished, uncollected, unsubmitted,
but not yet burnt. Or flooded. Or simply
given the hackerman's toss. I have every
reason to trust My Editor's taste. Obviously.

* * *

Bliss like mine took years. The time when I still
thought, maybe, maybe, I could win the love
of Max Goldberg. I tried both traditions:
faith and good works. Neither did. By "crafting"
letters, penning and crafting, I tried to create
intimacy without propinquity. It was never,
as they say, on the cards. Rose in dementia
liked holding a baby doll. Max suggested
naming the doll Sadie. His mother Sarah
had been a Sadie in her heyday. Are there any
activities at the synagogue he might enjoy?
I have arranged my decisions. Clearly, I have.
I am alone. I survey, before my presbyopic
eyes at the moment, a chunk of notebook
that somehow made it onto my hard drive.
Through multitudinous seasons, years, semesters
has this forgotten passage blushed unseen.
Laptop upon laptop, Mac this, Mac that.
In the margin, I now see, I word-processed
an interrogatory — I considered it brilliant then,

consider it jejune now — "Lucky or unlucky?" —
about the one person in a generation
who outlives all of his or her peers. Which
newspaper did your family take? What parish
gathered — prolonged — your affiliation?
Did your father go to Temple or to Shul?
What kind of penny candy was ubiquitous?
Does anyone here remember Arbor Day?

* * *

Frequently I fail in the gratitude catégory.
And shame on me for it. But thank you,
Providence, for this page of pixels, page of light,
trimmed with miniature icons, bordered by a ruler,
signposting potential: File, Edit, View, Insert —
I just this minute heard, as I do most days,
a mockingbird in the yaupon holly tree beyond
my open garage door. I am slow. I am grateful,
though, that I kept myself busy transcribing stuff
when I was in one long process of breaking
my heart, because — Eureka! A "poem" "found" —
vestige rendered — by vicissitude and by recognition —
whole. What's he going to do? Play cards with other
old men? It starts In Medias Res, the res being
a lost booklet or brochure of some kind
that came with the game of Rook, setting forth
rules for playing it, in sundry variations.
My extant text is fragmentary, truncated at the top,
but that's okay; it's plenty for getting the gist:

* * *

Poem

. . . so as to acquire a book
consisting of four cards of the same number.
The player who manages to do so quietly
puts his cards down, and folds his hands
in his lap. As soon as any other player
notes that one player has completed
a book of four cards, he quietly lays down
his cards, folding his hands in his lap.
The player who first gets four cards
of one kind is the Winner of the Game.
The very last player to fold his hands
must run around the table three times
calling "I am slow, I am slow."

* * *

Proof

of the same number. The player who manages to do so quietly puts his cards down, and folds his hands in his lap.

As soon as any other player notes that one player has completed a set of four cards, he quietly lays down his cards, folding his hands in his lap. The player who first gets four cards of any one kind is the winner of the game. The very last player to fold his hands must run around the table three times calling "I am slow, I am slow."

CLOCK PASTIME

For a single player

Deal one card at a time, face down, in a circle made up of 12 cards begining at the top, dealing two cards to the center to represent the clock hands. Continue dealing out the cards, four in each pile, all face down, until none are left.

Turn up the TOP CARD of the pile which is in the position of 1 o'clock. If this happens to be a 5, for example, place it face up at the bottom of the pile that is in the 5 o'clock position. If it is a 6, place it in the 6 o'clock position. Then turn up the upper card of the pile under which you have just placed a card, and place that card in the same manner in its proper pile, face up, on the

bottom of that pile. Continue this until all cards are turned up and placed into their proper numerical position. If the game works out, all the 13 and 14 cards will be in the middle piles and all other cards will be placed numerically on the piles around the clock, each identical numbered pile of cards in the proper position of the hours.

ROOK CLUBS AND TOURNAMENTS

Rook Clubs and Tournaments are becoming increasingly popular in many parts of the country. If you would be interested in learning more about Rook activities in your area, write to Parker Brothers, P. O. Box 900, Salem, Massachusetts 01970.

Any inquiries regarding the rules in this book, will be answered gladly by Parker Brothers, Salem, Mass. 01970.

PLEASE DO NOT TOUCH
OR LEAN ON THE RED
POLES IN THE THEATRE
AS THEY ARE PART OF
THE SET AND ARE NOT
STRUCTURAL! THANKS!

Fourth Board

But though they hurry so
To yield me mine, I shall not know
How well my want they'll have supplied
When notified.

Dirge for an Antiquated Practice in the Book Trade

ERRATUM

she lives there still page fourteen:
Hindu
should read:
Hindi

ERRATUM

the distaff side page fifty-nine:
Bodon
should read:
Bodoni

ERRATA

red signature page twenty-five:
partnerless in the last row
should read:
partnerless in the seat behind the driver

red signature page fifty-three:
nectarine
should read:
apricot

ERRATUM

finding the comfrey page two:
in this / precise / time
should read:
in this / precise / place

John and Charles

Chapter One

John Hargrove had a place out near Lone Chimney, Oklahoma, or as folks pronounced it, Long Chimbly. John was held to be a smart man, but lacking in ambition. Pretty much the only thing he liked about the place was the feel of the reins in his hands whenever he got off it.

Now for all that John neglected any job involving a hammer and a nail, in fairness, he did beautifully mind both his horses and their tack. He was proud to ride, or, if supplies needed getting, drive the buckboard into Pawnee, the bustling county seat. He usually dodged Old Man Berry, the banker, but enjoyed passing the time of day with whatever men were on the courthouse bench or in the barbershop.

His boy Charles was smart and ambitious, both. He wasn't all that interested in farming either, but he did bring a certain focus to his chores before school, and again after supper. Charles was called "Charlie" by both parents. He called John "Pops" and called Nancy, not "Moms" but "Mother." Nancy was usually the one scattering the chicken feed and shooing the rooster and gathering the eggs in the basket, except whenever she was poorly, Charlie took care of it.

Not since before Charles was born had Nancy attempted raising geese, and she even tried turkeys, for a spell. She would tell him, her only child, "Them birds were half-wild, and durned if they didn't go to roost up yonder [pointing to the crab-apple tree] or on the silo or pretty much wherever they wanted!" He said, "I never seen no chicken fly." She said, "Chickens cain't but turkeys can, a little ways."

Chapter Two

One school-day during morning chores, Charlie felt a case of diarrhea coming on, and landed up in the privy for the second time since breakfast.

"Hurry up, Charlie!" John shouted from the driver's seat of the buckboard. "You're gonna be tardy!"

The boy in his haste did a not-very-good job wiping himself with a page torn from the weather-curled Sears & Roebuck catalog.

The upshot was, whenever John left Charlie off at the schoolyard that day, the Pawnee Indian kids bunched up around him, pointing at him, holding their noses or waving their hands in front of their faces, regaling themselves:

"Oooooo. Kuh-da si-tka-ha!" which means, not to put too fine a point on it, "shitty ass."

Charlie, though, was a good-natured culprit, and he laughed along. "Kit-spus" he said, meaning "maybe a little bit."

Chapter Three

Lone Chimney School covered grades 1-8. Plenty of boys left school at nine or ten to help — in some cases to be — the man of the house. Not Charlie. Nancy wouldn't hear of it. And neither, truth be told, would John.

More girls than boys succeeded in completing eighth grade. But few rural scholars of either gender matriculated at the castle-like High School in Pawnee. Charlie was one of that minority. He was pretty much a straight-A student and he went out for basketball, too.

At that time, the Pawnee Bruins had one coach and six players. Charlie was not tallest, or second tallest, or third tallest, but he was motivated and quick, made a good point guard. Seldom was he the one boy on the bench while the other five covered the court.

Miss Clara Bateman, P.H.S.'s most formidable teacher, he thought of as old, but really she was middle-aged. English was not Charlie's favorite subject; chemistry was. Anyway, whenever Miss Bateman was, in fact, old, Charlie's own kids had her for English. She told each and every one of them, year by year, "Your father was far and away the most intelligent boy I ever taught at Pawnee High School."

At graduation, Charlie — at that time, Miss Bateman was alone in calling him "Charles" — gave the valedictory address. Nancy was all smiles. Unashamed, she blotted tears from her cheeks with her hankie. Miss Bateman had a hankie on her too, of course, but she didn't need it on that particular occasion. As for John, sure, he felt emotion but, as men do, whenever they feel tears fixing to come up in their eyes, they keep them from falling by clamping their lips shut tight.

Chapter Four

Come Labor Day, Charlie took the northbound Santa Fe line and arrived in Lawrence to become a Kansas Jayhawk, not in Basketball or Chemistry, but in Biology. College was tougher than high school but he maintained a B+ average over the four years.

Summers he spent at home. Come the June after college graduation, one afternoon found Charlie sitting at the kitchen table. John was off to town as per usual. Nancy was lying down upstairs to rest her eyes, which was what she called sleeping during the day. Charlie filled his ink-pen. He had a pencil and a scratch-pad handy, too, for thinking, plus a business envelope ready with two stamps, since the document he was going to send was thick when folded up.

He took great care, then, filling out his application for the new medical school in St. Louis at Washington University. After he finished the form, he signed it, ritually, with his full name — Charles Hugh Hargrove. The wooden tabletop was inscribed with scratches and discolorations but they were so familiar, Charlie paid them no mind.

What he did notice, though, was that, for some reason, the burring sound the locusts made in the cottonwood tree seemed extra loud, loud to where the sound and the windless heat were part and parcel of one passing thing.

Chapter Five

Charles Hugh Hargrove was turned down at first. But his response was to refold the rejection letter, get on the train in Pawnee, get off in St. Louis, present himself in person to the Dean of Admissions.

He impressed upon the man how hard it had been as a child to listen to and watch his mother, with her severe asthma, frantic whenever she went to draw breath and could hardly do it, and flat worn out besides. "I swore then and there," he said, "that whenever I grew up, I would be a doctor so's I could stop people having to suffer like that."

The Dean said, "I'll have to talk to some people." The Dean said, "Do you have somewhere you could stay till Monday?" Charlie said "Yessir" which was not quite true, not yet, but he had pictured the boarding house he noticed walking to campus. Immediately he left the Dean's office, he went straight there.

"Yes," said the lady, "I always have plenty of rooms in the Summer, but I'm full up when school's on. Do you want to reserve a room for the Fall?"

"I don't know yet, ma'am. I hope so." He blushed. "Do you mind telling me the cost?"

Lo and behold, Charlie left St. Louis with his room reserved and his first semester's books purchased along with a satchel to hold them. On the train, he started in to studying, turning first to Bass's The History of Medicine: deep-dyed blue covers and dense print and thin pages, charts and graphs and line illustrations of things like the microscope and bacteria, figures of Hippocrates in Greece and Galen in Rome.

In Pawnee, John met him at the station. No longer in the buckboard. In a Model-T Ford automobile, with his son's Western Union telegram on the dashboard. For the first time, John and Charles shook hands, as men.

Chapter Six

Over the following years, the smart and ambitious Hargrove used his study habits to make decent grades in his classes, but where he most excelled was in the Internship, then the Residency. During that last year, he made friends with a fellow Resident, a St. Louis man, who took to bringing Charles along for Sunday dinner, which was what they called supper.

That was where he met the girl he was to marry, not without honorably making it clear it would mean living in his hometown out in Oklahoma.

He said, "It can get awful dusty."

She said, "Well, it sounds awfully charming to me."

Even before he and Mary moved into their first house, on Elm Street, Charles obtained his Oklahoma Medical License, signed and sealed, to add to his signed-and-sealed diploma from Washington University College of Medicine.

He had them both professionally framed. No stranger to hammer and nail, Charles hung his certificates side-by-side on the pale-green cinderblock wall above his new oak desk. The office he had rented on the north side of the town Square was three doors down from the office of the one other physician in Pawnee, name of Earl Buchanan.

Dr. Buchanan ridiculed and belittled his own grown sons in public. He turned that same treatment on the whipper-snapper Charles H. Hargrove, M.D. To no avail. Pretty much everybody switched to Charlie, ever after called Doc.

By and by, Doc Hargrove practiced medicine in two capacities, as the main doctor in Pawnee, and on top of that, upon appointment by the United States Department of the Interior to head the federal hospital built to serve the Pawnee, as well as the Ponca, the Otoe, and the Tonkawa.

Chapter Seven

"Ever-body dance!" calls out the Master of Ceremonies over the staticky loud-speaker at the Annual Pawnee Indian Veterans Homecoming Powwow. The call gives rise to communal round-dances, which take place in casual intervals among the exacting competitive dances. The drum makes a central hub. Singer/drummers sit in a ring around it facing inward toward the music.

The round dance mingles all ages, some holding babies, or toddlers by the hand. Into orbit come more and more dancer/walkers, facing forward in a left-to-right direction of rotation. They form clusters, not lanes or spokes. Girls and women, even if wearing modern clothes, will all have their shawl with them, or borrow one.

They learn to make the long fringe sway to the rhythm. By the way, instead of stomping each foot twice as the men do — left left right right left left right right — women put in a little dip, slightly bending knees, both feet on the ground — left dip right dip left dip right dip. They might add in a traditional beaded bag on a wrist, or hold a fan of feathers, overlapped and lashed to the handle, just so.

Whenever a man gets too old for the time-honored masculine double-stomp in forward motion, he can always stay in near the drum-circle and keep to the pattern in a stationery form, tapping only his heels — left left right right left left right right left left right right. . . .

Chapter Eight

Up to the end of his long career, whenever Doc Hargrove walked into the Indian Hospital, the people around his age would greet him with a grin and a pointing finger, "kuh-da si-tka-ha!" He'd grin back and say "kit-spus." Ever-body laugh. . . .

But back to John Hargrove. Charlie's gift of the gab wasn't a patch on his old man's. Naturally, a lot of folks had John

Hargrove in their stories. He was seldom dubbed "a good old boy," but frequently, "a character," or less charitably, "a piece of work." For sure he delighted in folk expressions such as "Come hell or high water," and its cousin, "God willing and the creek don't rise."

He even had sayings a doctor might could use. "That went like a dose of salts through a widow-woman." Or in a case where the end is drawing nigh, "She ain't gone, but she's circling the drain." Or for a man with advanced dementia, "He don't know get-up from sic-em."

John never reached the dementia stage, died from a massive heart attack at fifty-four. So he never got to have the full pride of knowing how well his boy did, making a good living doing work he was cut out for, work he loved.

But if John were to know, beyond the burials of all concerned, about that school-yard comedy, shared so many decades after it occurred, and last shared still more decades counting back from today, he may have said, "Now that's a picture no artist could paint":

Charles (fingers bent by arthritis to match the angled medical scissors in his shirt pocket) and the then-Elders of the Pawnee Nation (eyes crinkled, voices throaty, mouths wide, some more gums than teeth) — everybody laughing — laughing with such pleasure.

Spire and Dove*

I.

Noon and the bird watches the sun converge
with the green intelligence of tree-leaves.
I pluck the white sphere, the moon-white sphere, filled
with gaps, centered on dark-brown oblong seeds.

Yes, familiar sphere: dandelion seeds.
I hold it by the stalk, proffer it up,
shift it forwards and back as if using
the hand lens, to superimpose (my point

of view) the penumbra upon the bird.
Not halo, mind, the bird is more subtly
divine. When wind comingles grist and air,
I wear, willingly, their veil. Toward the green

intelligence of the dandelion's
launchpad, I puff *who, whoo. Whhhoo.* It takes me
three tries. I tilt my head. The bird tilts its
head. It flies. It today has got to eat.

Is the life-force all of it? part of it?
both? What perpetual ephemera
lets it know, as each eye-bright being must:
grass roots steer worms and worms make dirt of dust.

*ERRATA:
"Spire" was actually neither a church steeple nor a microwave tower, but a radio
tower, not latticed, but held in place with guy wires
"Dove" was actually a mockingbird

Now it is one of the days when the sky,
rather than blue/gray or pink/orange, dawns white.
While I am driving on the highway, lost,
I see the microwave tower whose high tip

keeps flashing, flashing the same hue of white
as the sky, such that the star-like pin-point
is barely visible, or invisible,
absent, or dim, through the thin cloud-cover.

Other drivers (I refocus, glimpse them)
seem bent on getting somewhere, unaware
(as far as I can tell) of the beacon.
Is that how it is with the holy ghost?

Appearance tiny, retained in the frame;
the cinematographer implying *No,
you are not lost.* Though I think I am
perched on the mere cusp of change, the change thinks

otherwise. The sun does not hesitate
because it is obscured. Cirrus clouds form
high, cumulus low, enfolding the flash,
cradling meaning beamed from the spear-made gash.

Fifth Board

Those boards and I — how much
In common we, of feel and touch
Shall share thence on, — earth's far core-quakings,
Hill-shocks, tide-shakings —

Three Songs from Nebraska

Bride

He explained in his letter
The prairie is Nebraska's ocean
I hail from the Gulf Coast
And cannot figure this out

The prairie is Nebraska's ocean
I get mixed up not knowing
And cannot figure this out
How to measure the snowflakes

I get mixed up not knowing
Since they come in two sizes
How to measure the snowflakes
Some fall and some hover

Since they come in two sizes
Like mosquitoes and gnats
Some fall and some hover
In speeds I cannot predict

Like mosquitoes and gnats
I remember from the summer
In speeds I cannot predict
In wind I cannot read

I remember from the summer
He explained in his letter
In wind I cannot read
I hail from the Gulf Coast

Wife

What with the sun
What with the time
What with lye soap
My cotton white hands

Have turned out red
What with the sun
What with the dust
What with sparing the soap

My red gingham curtains
Have turned out gray
What with time sheer time
My once red hair

Has turned out white
'Stead of ugly old gray
For that I am glad
At one with the sun

Widow

Let the Manheim Motor Parts calendar blur
Let its picture of happy mountain goats fade
Let the pencil's string turn from white to gray
And let the notations — moot now — blanch

His quick writing, left-handed, back-sloping
3:30 — Doc Hargrove — Hearing Test
Tractors make for loud work. I could spot him
From away far off by the list of his gait

His old fedora, sweat for a hatband. . . . Sleeves
Rolled up past his elbows, hands. . . . enlarged
. . . .
How he lathered them gray with Lava soap. . . .

. . . .
I will not disturb the pencil, no, nor will I
Flip the page. The year stays up there, one hole
Punched through twelve months, suspended
. . . .
. . . .

From the nail he hammered into the door
Of the broom closet and painted around
Last time he repainted. The iron nail rusts
Rusts, crumbles, reassembles as red ants

Double Visitation

2004 Honda Civic
country roads near
Norman, Oklahoma

One time, as I headed to the all-night
veterinary clinic with Lydia,
cat of nineteen years, to obtain a death

for her, sweet dainty cat, and shy, being
driven away from home, as dark floated
for ten seconds or so above first light. . . .

One time, as I headed home from a good
long talk with a friend, as last light lingered
for ten seconds or so below new night. . . .

Both times, my mother swooped over my car,
so low I flinched at such a fast gliding
shape. But what it was — an owl — registered

only in two seconds' retrospect. Now,
retrospect on retrospect, I still think
her mind somehow reached mine. In a single

intake of breath without means of letting
it out. Subjects without means of predicates.
She had been saying   *mist afloat in oak trees*

saying   *feathery spray of blood*   saying
buffalo skull in white alkaline sun's
template   then, then, *gentle scent of pollen*

and slide of water spider. . . . A thousand
thousand nominals saying what she knew:
The world is very old and shallow breathes —

916 Oakbrook Drive
Norman, Oklahoma
Winter 2021

Still, I grieve for Lydia, whose formal
name, by the way, was rarely used in life.
She knew she was loved as "Liddle Lyddy."

If, then, some sad time hence, you should happen
upon my elegy titled "Double
Visitation," know that Owl's messages,

delivered in italics, descend from
various works of the largely unknown
poet, Katharine H. Privett, my mother.

Glen Gathering
Asheville, North Carolina
Summer 2022

Mother, great news! The workshop really loved
all your language, especially the line
where I revealed (by fiddling with your line-

breaks, ha!) "found" iambic pentameter,
"enhancing" your beautiful poesis:
The world is very old [/] and shallow breathes.

Listen as I quote

Long Illness

> She moves her colored pills around
> as God, his stars and planets:
> days, counted and contained.
>
> She hears the clock tick all night long;
> the program of its logic
> lodges in her brain.
>
> She watches dry weeds in the wind,
> fields that shrink before
> the cold and winnowing.
>
> She knows the world is very old
> and shallow breathes. As blade
> to whetstone, on and on,
>
> its sleep is shaped. By invalid
> routines, she cuts pain's tongue
> until it cannot speak.

Attribute as I unquote   — Katharine H. Privett (1924–1995)
                                          Winter 1991

Owl who, silent, sweeps
Winter 2037

Who, pray, was the "she" in "Long Illness"? I
cannot tell you. I do not know. Mother
watched many women enduring long illness,

sure she endured such herself, and she died
some time ago. Years younger than myself.
No asking the poet to name names now.

Interrupted Chant

breathes the world is very old and shallow (breathes
the world is very old and shallow breathes (the
world is very old and shallow breathes the (world

is very old and shallow breathes the world (is
very old and shallow breathes the world is (ve-
ry old and shallow breathes the world is ve (ry

old and shallow breathes the world is very (old
and shallow breathes the world is very old (and
shallow breathes the world is very old and (shal-

Annunciation; or, Memory*

* When I was nineteen — the summer of 1967, it was — I had a student job in
the library at Oklahoma State University. My main employment was running the
newly established xerox room, located in more-or-less a closet, which had been
claimed from a remote corner of the vast fourth floor and outfitted with heavy-
duty electrical outlets for the purpose.

The library's one photocopier was in fact not a Xerox machine but a European
model, an Olivetti, that used liquid toner instead of powder. I was there to make
copies for customers at a small charge. This was slightly before coin-operated
models showed up on each floor of the library. And anyway, using 3x5 index cards
to track research was still by far the dominant methodology of scholars, so I did
not do a very brisk business.

With lots of free time, then, and no supervision (being hundreds of tall
bookstacks away from the central glassed-in island of librarians), I made images
for fun. It has been fifty-seven years, but some survived — iterations of iterations
for the most part — including the sequence of self-portraits presented here as
plates. I've spliced among them verses from the Book of Luke, as translated in *The
Jerusalem Bible*, edition of 1966.

— M. L.

In the sixth month the angel Gabriel was sent by God to a town in Galilee called Nazareth, to a virgin betrothed to a man named Joseph, of the House of David; and the virgin's name was Mary.

— Luke 1:26-27

He went in and said to her, "Rejoice, so highly favored! The Lord is with you." She was deeply disturbed by these words and asked herself what this greeting could mean, but the angel said to her, "Mary, do not be afraid; you have won God's favor. Listen! You are to conceive and bear a son, and you must name him Jesus. He will be great and will be called Son of the Most High. The Lord God will give him the throne of his ancestor David; he will rule over the House of Jacob for ever and his reign will have no end."

— Luke 1:28-33

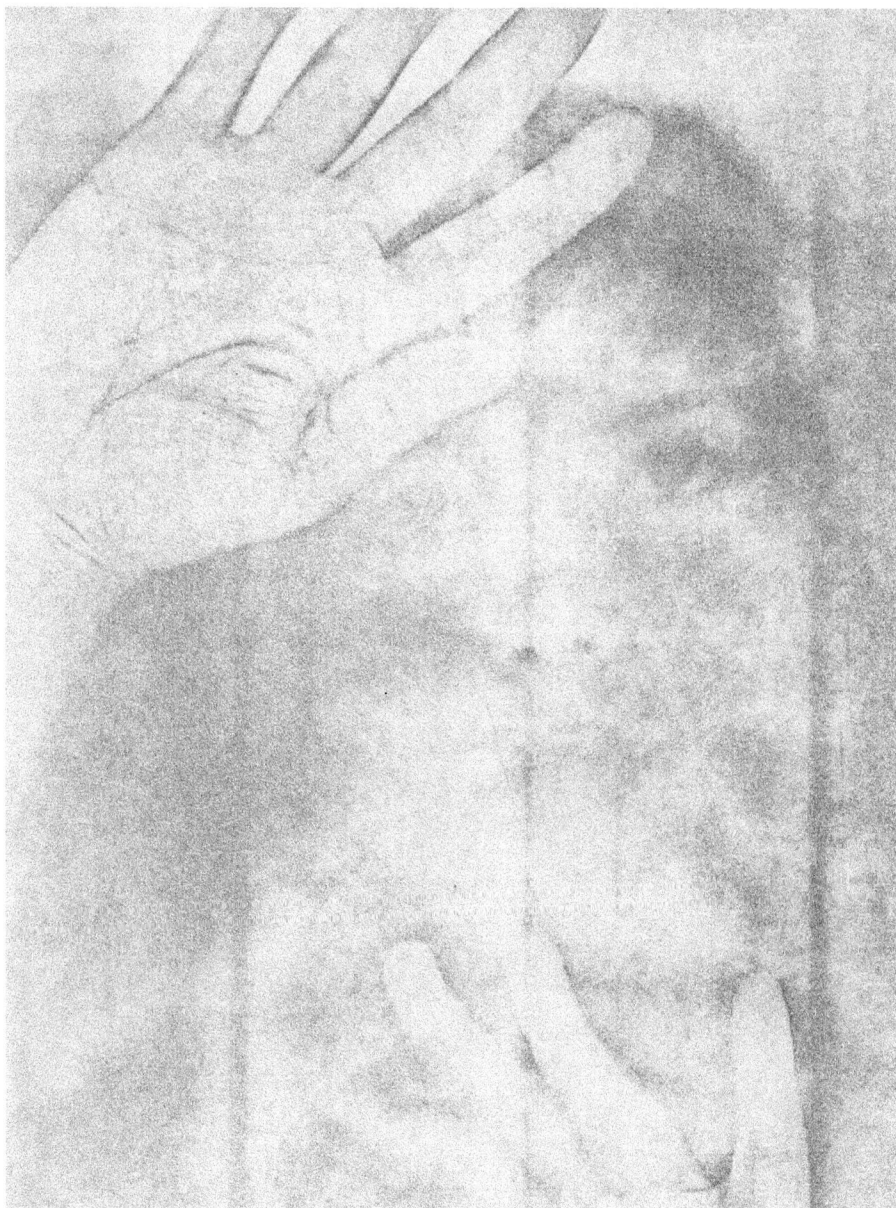

Mary said to the angel, "But how can this come about, since I am a virgin?" "The Holy Spirit will come upon you," the angel answered, "and the power of the Most High will cover you with its shadow."

— Luke 1: 34-35

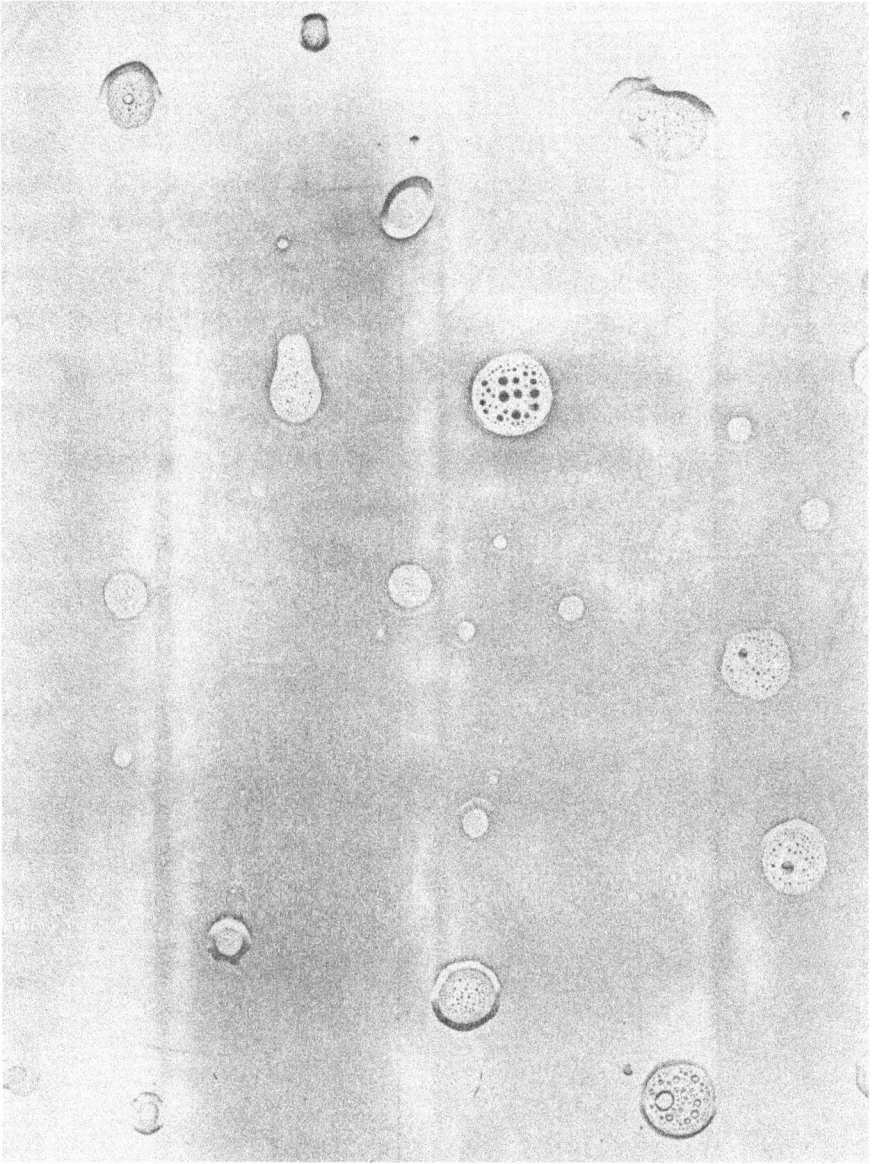

"*I am the handmaid of the Lord,*" said Mary, "*let what you have said be done to me.*"

— Luke 1:38 beginning of verse

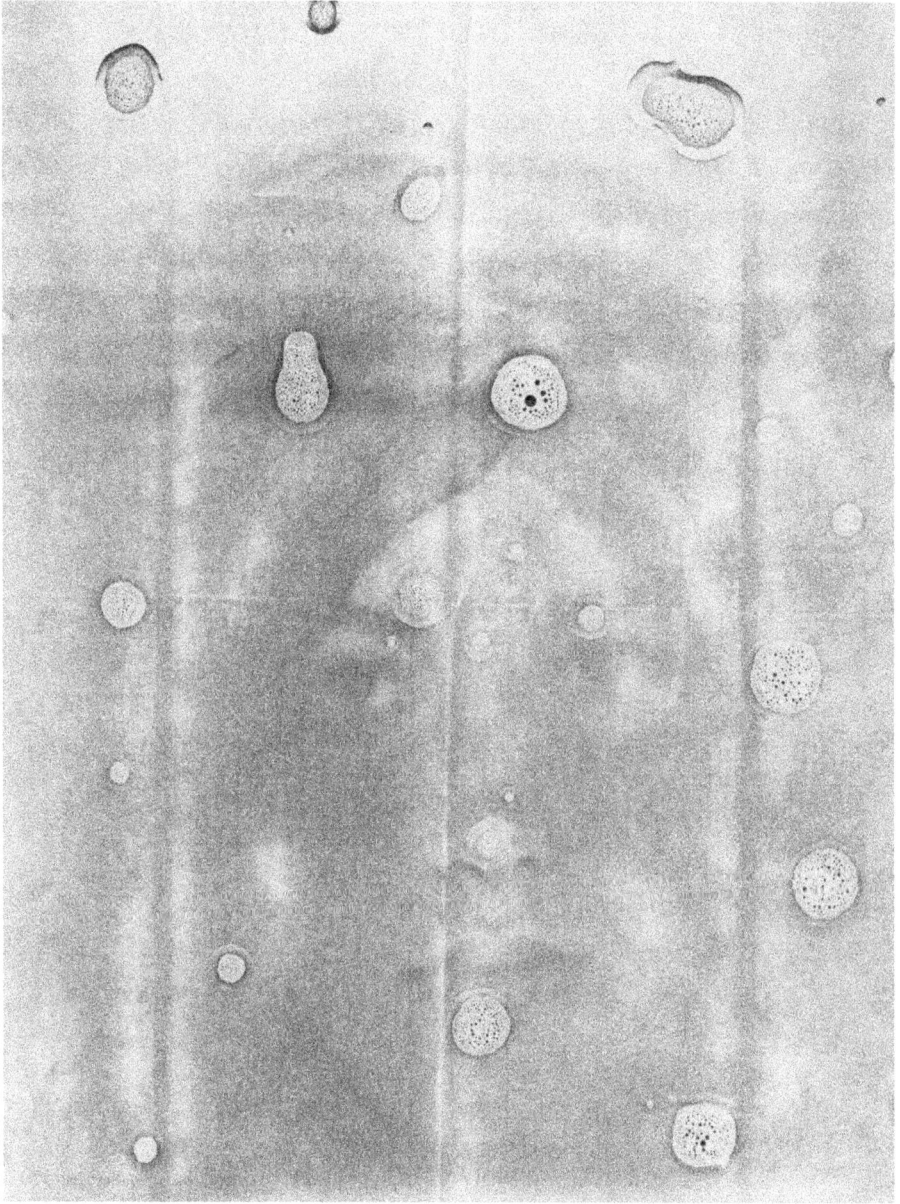

And the angel left her.

— Luke 1:38 conclusion of verse

The Lid

Yea, hid where none will note,
The once live tree and man, remote
From mundane hurt as if on Venus, Mars,
Or furthest stars.

The Methodist Ministry of Samuel Walsh Franklin

Day-Spring from on high, be near;
Day-Star, in my heart appear.
— Charles Wesley

> I dreamt I was out on a prairie
> > by an old buffalo wallow
> > that was fed by a cool, bubbling stream.
> On a stand before me
> > was a tall, clear, crystal pitcher
> > surrounded by twelve glasses.
> As people came along, I would offer them
> > a drink of water.
> Cowboys would ride by on their horses
> > and I would say,
> > "Will you have a drink of cool water?"
> They would get down off of their horses
> > and drink of the water.
> And then they would ride off to their work again,
> > refreshed.

The Sun

Behind every heresiarch, there is a woman.
— Eusebius Sophronius Hieronymus*

Tessa Rae knew not boredom. She could always
plumb the volume, *The Splendid Leopard of Infinite
Sigils.* This morning, she consulted it as to the forecast:
a delicious dark-clouded day, twilight at 1800 hours.
God, who was reading over her shoulder, said, "So,
woman, mind you shut the shutters perfectly, then."

God spoke the vulgate Latin in the library on account of
Jerome was known to pop in unannounced. Did she,
woman, shut the shutters perfectly? No. She did,
however, take the precaution of removing from
the windowsill a short beaker of water holding
a posy of shamrocks she picked on her way here.

While she was at it, she observed, through the unglazed
window, clouds and cloudiness in motion cohering.
Gigantic harbinger raindrops scatter-blasted her face.
She laughed when a barometric shift sucked suddenly
her pale gray gauze veil right off her head and out onto
the wind, where, kite-like, it bobbed to up fro down,

writing cursive. She remarked to God, "Nothing You
say will avert a deluge now." Unsure how to feel
about the wind getting away with misdemeanor theft,
she did go ahead and shut the shutters. Perfectly.
God sputtered, "Her effrontery!" Jerome appeared
in a flash of broad-brimmed straw hat and immediately

*Also known as Jerome of Stridon, Doctor of the Church, Patron Saint of
Translators, Librarians, Archivists, Researchers, Encylopædists, etc.

agreed with God in writing: *Silly women, burdened*
with sins, carried about with every wind of doctrine,
ever learning and never able to come to the knowledge
of the truth. Tessa Rae, admittedly guilty of ever
learning, texted her cousin Lizzie, "Who does he think
he is, dissing innocent wind like that? You know what?

I'm fine with the loss of my pale gray gauze veil."
She'd been pet-sitting for Jerome, too, gratis, although
she didn't complain. She was, actually, quite fond
of Keeper, his dalmatian, and his mutt, Flossie,
and especially, his big lion, Leonine. All three beasts
behaved very well in the reading room, observing

studious decorum, seldom jumping up on anybody.
As Jerome wrangled the gnarly knot of his chinstrap
loose and hung his hat on its peg, "Hmm," thought
Tessa Rae. The truth was, she liked the curmudgeon;
for example, she liked that, for the oldest books,
he went back to the Hebrew, instead of taking

seventy other dudes' word for it, their Greek,
like their backs, unmuscular. Next she thought,
"She must be busy," because Lizzie's reply text
consisted only of sigils for heart and for shamrock.
Tessa Rae had requested and received leave
to install a prie-dieu in her corner. On it, she kept,

not her copy of *The Virgin's Book*, but a substantial
white rock, water-carved over millennia to resemble
a skull of bovine origin, complete with water-carved
holes like eye-sockets for a gentle creature. Jerome
pulled his human skull from his rucksack, centered it
on his table, and sat down with his quill plus forty

reams of foolscap, which God Himself had provided
as part of Jerome's Post-Doc. The sun, having decided
to reschedule twilight, came out full and strong.
Tessa Rae opened the shutters, then chose from the wall
the embossed leather purse stuffed with correspondence
from Dr. Mirabilis, Friar Rodger [Bacon] to his friends.

She committed to memory some of his written words:
Words arrive from the interior of the person by reason
of the cogitation and desire of the soul and by reason
of the urge and heat of the spirit. God in His armchair
lounged, flipping through a portfolio of famous horses.
Now the sun assumed its antepenultimate slant

of the day. Tessa Rae made her way up the spiral
staircase, got several pounds of history, lugged them
to the nearest carrell. Sir Dairmaid's index: *Jerome,*
Errors of. She found herself resisting the glib tone
of the writing: *Some of his [Jerome's] mistranslations*
were more comic than important. One of the most

curious was Exodus 34:29 where the Hebrew describes
Moses's face as shining when he came down from
Mount Sinai bearing the Ten Commandments, Jerome,
mistaking particles of Hebrew, turned this into
Moses wearing a pair of horns, and so the Lawgiver
is frequently depicted in Christian art, long after

humanists gleefully removed the horns from the text.
Tessa Rae knew this passage would hurt Jerome's
feelings, so when she returned Sir D to the stacks,
she misshelved him. Back in her seat downstairs,
she looked at Jerome across the room, and thought,
"He's doing his level best." The sun, now, assumed

its penultimate slant of the day. God arose and said,
"I think I'll take Keeper and Flossie walkies,"
and He sorted the leashes. "H'rtraw!" said or barked
each of the three as, alertly, they departed the west door,
fading into light. Tessa Rae did a few neckrolls,
clockwise and counter. The sun assumed its ultimate

slant of the day now. Jerome wouldn't
look up from his work. Tessa Rae couldn't
catch his eye. On the worn flagstone floor, in a last
patch of warmth, lay Leonine, mellowing out,
mouth full of drowse, and tongue, and peace,
his closed eyelids resembling swung dashes ~ ~

Circles

∞X∞

Tara proposed that we meditate upon
our future selves, our most highly evolved, wise,
   compassionate selves down the road, say, five years,
      ten years, twenty-five years! I was seventy-
         six at the time and knew how to add. Tara
      went on, "Imagine where your future self lives,
   even what you're wearing." (Now I'm interested.)
Stripes, and their O.C.D. children, tartans, said
   my cloth mind. Florals came and went. When I asked
      my beau to choose one of two scarves, he chose stripes
         over flowers. Of the flowered exemplar,
      he adjudged: "Too many colors." But, then, he
   worked in stripes, didn't he. A mower. And I
was not genuinely prepared to reject
   every last floral or too many colors
      on his say-so. When in my sixties, I said
         "white" rarely, often "green." When in my eighties,
      it was quite the reverse. Either way, solids
   monochromatic head to toe, and in this,
was like Queen Elizabeth, whether the First
   or the Second of the name, announcing "Blue!"
      or "Melon!" and on the instant, it was done.
         For my seventies, that tired adolescence,
      I gravitated to heather, or marling,
   blends of two colors, or a color and white,
or a color and black, which appear solid
   from a distance but highly textured up close.

∞Y∞

Our eighteen-year-olds, our eighty-one-year-olds,
marvel at each other's skin. Both try to find

adjectives. The young say "papery." The old
say "dewy." She of skin-soft-as-bluebonnets

cannot remotely envisage looking like
she of wrinkles-ancestrally-written, who

thinks back to her own innocent losses.
"I don't," as me auld mither say'd tae meself,

"feel any different inside." We, all ourselves,
live simultaneously. Now, at ninety,

as I traverse Etsy, I type in "abstract"
and hit search, designated by a spy glass!

I type "geometric." Search. Then "medallion."
Ditto. No series of closely spaced dots, called

a line, knows, flowing in real time, whether it's
headed straight or crisscross, spiral or paisley.

∞Z∞

If I return to wearing love-beads, head-bands,

Bell-bottom blue-jeans *(I sewed trim, broad jacquard*

Ribbon, to the leg hems, which dragged the ground

Underneath my thin-soled buckskin moccasins) —

A blouse, with drawstring closures, at neck and wrists

— *(I embroidered it with blossoming morning-*

Glory vines and contemporary peace signs

And pointy hearts) — an ending looms. Then make my

Bed, Little Sister. Make it long and narrow.

Appendix

The Six Boards

Six boards belong to me:
I do not know where they may be;
If growing green or lying dry
            In a cockloft nigh.

Some morning I shall claim them,
And who may then possess will aim them
To bring me those boards I need
            With thoughtful speed.

But though they hurry so
To yield me mine, I shall not know
How well my want they'll have supplied
            When notified.

Those boards and I—how much
In common we, of feel and touch
Shall share thence on, — earth's far core-quakings —
            Hill-shocks, tide-shakings —

Yea, hid where none will note,
The once live tree and man, remote:
From mundane hurt as if on Venus, Mars,
            Or furthest stars.

— Thomas Hardy (1840-1928)*

*On 16th January 1928, the ashes of Thomas Hardy were buried in Poets' Corner in Westminster Abbey. But his heart is buried at Stinsford in Dorset, where his parents lie.

The Hardy Tree

A young Thomas Hardy's first profession was architecture, which he achieved by apprenticeship, and then pursued in London. One of the projects he worked on there in 1862 entailed excavating a portion of the burial ground at St Pancras, Old Church, ahead of an extension of the Midland Railway cutting through the site.

A bunch of headstones ended up abandoned. In later years, the stones became situated in legend where they stood, stacked like books encircling a vigorous ash tree. As the notion grew that Hardy himself had arranged the stones against the tree, the name "The Hardy Tree" got attached to the striking landmark, and so it has remained through many a civic tour and literary pilgrimage.

Aftermath: the ash, having contracted a deadly fungus, had its crown trimmed back so as to limit the area around it, preventing harm to visitors in case the tree fell, which, during Christmastide of 2022, happened. Erratum: photographic history has established that the stones were there first. Only sometime after 1926 did the tree, evidently, self-seed within the configuration.

Those developments are immaterial to the writer of the pieces collected here. Rather, the idea of root and rock comingling endures as an emblem.

References:

Bingham, David. *The London Dead: Stories from our cemeteries, crypts and churchyards.* "The Myth of the Hardy Tree; Old St Pancras Churchyard." 25 April 2021. https://thelondondead.blogspot.com/2021/04/the-myth-of-hardy-tree-old-st-pancras.html

Gross, Jenny. "The Hardy Tree, a Beloved Fixture of a London Cemetery, Topples Over." *The New York Times*, 28 Dec 2022. https://www.nytimes.com/2022/12/28/world/europe/hardy-tree-london.html

Editorial. "The Guardian view on the death of the Hardy Tree: a legend uprooted." *The Guardian*, 29 Dec 2022. https://www.theguardian.com/commentisfree/2022/dec/29/the-guardian-view-on-the-death-of-the-hardy-tree-a-legend-uprooted

Carrier, Dan. "Forget everything you thought you knew about 'The Hardy Tree'." *Camden New Journal*, 14 April 2023. https://www.camdennewjournal.co.uk/article/forget-everything-you-thought-you-knew-from-the-hardy-tree

On the cover: Photo by Paul Hudson with enhancements, licensed under Creative Commons 2.0.

Author photo courtesy of Margaret Ann Wadleigh.

Design by Tony Roberts

www.ingramcontent.com/pod-product-compliance
Lightning Source LLC
Chambersburg PA
CBHW022159080426
42734CB00006B/506